postcards from new zealand

First published in 2011 by Craig Potton Publishing
98 Vickerman Street, PO Box 555, Nelson, New Zealand
www.craigpotton.co.nz

© Bob McCree

ISBN 978 1 877517 47 1

Printed in China by Midas Printing International Ltd

postcards from new zealand

Bob McCree

craig potton publishing

Te Werahi Beach and Cape Maria Van Diemen, Northland

Cape Reinga Lighthouse, Northland

Whananaki Coastal Walk near Tutukaka, Northland

Tane Mahuta, New Zealand's largest kauri tree, Northland

The Stone Store, New Zealand's oldest stone building, Kerikeri, Northland

Te Whare Runanga, the carved Maori Meeting House at Waitangi, Bay of Islands

Piha Beach with Lion Rock, West Auckland

Anawhata Beach, West Auckland
FOLLOWING PAGES Sunset over the centre of Auckland City

Westhaven Marina, Auckland

A paraglider above North Head, Devonport, Auckland, with Rangitoto Island behind

Auckland City at night, seen from Stanley Point, Devonport

The *Dawn Princess* leaving Auckland City

Sandy Bay on Waiheke Island, Hauraki Gulf

The Yesteryear Barn near Paeroa, Waikato

Torehina Bay, Coromandel Peninsula

Camping on the beach, Port Jackson, Coromandel Peninsula

Dairy cows near Arapuni, South Waikato

Mt Kakepuku and farmland, seen from near Te Awamutu, Waikato

Waireinga/Bridal Veil Falls near Raglan, Waikato

A stream in native forest near Waitomo, South Waikato

Carving on a Maori Meeting House at Ohinemutu, Rotorua

Rotorua Museum of Art and History, Rotorua

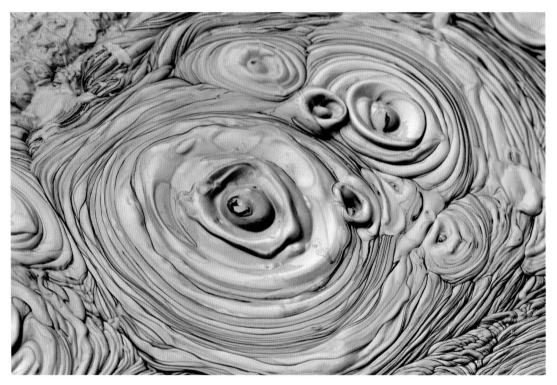

A hot mud pool in the geothermal area at Waiotapu, near Rotorua

Pohutu Geyser, Te Whakarewarewa Thermal Valley, Rotorua

Trout in a pool at the Rainbow Springs Kiwi Wildlife Park, Rotorua

Lake Tarawera, near Rotorua

A yacht on a calm morning, Lake Taupo

Sheep graze under Mt Ruapehu, near Ohakune, Central North Island
FOLLOWING PAGES Winter snow on Mts Ngauruhoe and Tongariro, Tongariro National Park

Whakapapa Skifield, Mt Ruapehu, Tongariro National Park

Evening at the Chateau Tongariro, Mt Ruapehu, Tongariro National Park

The Tawhai Falls on the Whakapapanui Stream, Tongariro National Park

Mts Tongariro and Ngauruhoe, Tongariro National Park

Hill country near Taumarunui, King Country

A mob of sheep in front of the remote Whangamomona Hotel, on the
Forgotten World Highway, inland Taranaki

Evening light on Mt Taranaki, from near Oaonui, Taranaki

Sea cliffs at Tongaporutu, northern Taranaki

Mt Taranaki from North Egmont, Egmont National Park

Cape Egmont Lighthouse, with Mt Taranaki behind, Taranaki

The historic main street of Mangaweka, Manawatu

Corrugated iron gumboot sculpture, the motif of Taihape, Rangitikei

Lake Waikaremoana, Te Urewera National Park

Makorori Beach, Gisborne

Art Deco building in Hastings, Hawke's Bay

Art Deco hotel, Napier, Hawke's Bay

Farmland above Waimarama Beach, Hawke's Bay

Black Barn Vineyard near Havelock North, Hawke's Bay

Gannet colony at Cape Kidnappers, Hawke's Bay

Castlepoint Lighthouse, Wairarapa

The Beehive, the Executive Wing of Parliament Buildings, Wellington

New Zealand Parliament Buildings, Wellington

Chaffers Marina and hillside houses, Oriental Bay, Wellington

Museum of New Zealand Te Papa Tongarewa, and Circa Theatre, Wellington

The Interislander Cook Strait ferry entering Tory Channel, Marlborough Sounds

Te Ranui Bay, Queen Charlotte Sounds, Marlborough Sounds

Vineyards near Seddon in the Awatere Valley, Marlborough

Vineyard in the Lower Awatere Valley, Marlborough

Summer on Tahunanui Beach, Nelson

Christ Church Cathedral and the Church Steps, Nelson

The golden sands of Totaranui Beach, Abel Tasman National Park

Summer at Kaiteriteri Beach, Nelson

Tata Beach, Golden Bay

Kerr Bay, Lake Rotoiti, Nelson Lakes National Park

Evening light at Kaikoura, with the Seaward Kaikoura Range behind

New Zealand fur seal, Kaikoura

Coastline near Kekerengu, with the Seaward Kaikoura Range above, Marlborough

Caravan selling crayfish, north of Kaikoura

Christchurch Art Gallery, with tram, Christchurch

The Avon River flowing through the Botanic Gardens, Christchurch

Church Bay, Lyttelton Harbour, Banks Peninsula

Wharf, Akaroa Harbour, Banks Peninsula

Limestone outcrops at Castle Hill, Canterbury high country

A mob of sheep on the move near Motunau, North Canterbury

Jacks Hut, a historic roadman's cottage near Arthur's Pass

Railway shed at Cass in the Canterbury high country, the subject of the famous painting *Cass*, by Rita Angus

Devils Punchbowl Waterfall, Arthur's Pass National Park

New Zealand's rare alpine parrot, the kea, Arthur's Pass National Park

Lake Tekapo and the Southern Alps from the altar window of the
Church of the Good Shepherd, Tekapo, Mackenzie Country

Autumn at Lake Alexandrina, Mackenzie Country
FOLLOWING PAGES Winter morning on a hydro canal near Twizel, Mackenzie Country

East Face of Mt Sefton, Aoraki/Mount Cook National Park

Evening on Lake Pukaki, with Aoraki/Mt Cook behind, Mackenzie Country

The South Face of Aoraki/Mt Cook from the Hooker Valley,
Aoraki/Mount Cook National Park

The statue of Sir Edmund Hillary at the Hermitage, Mount Cook

Victorian limestone buildings in the historic precinct, Oamaru

Huriawa Pa historic site, near Karitane, North Otago

The Moeraki Boulders, North Otago

The Purakaunui Falls, the Catlins, South Otago

A still morning on the Otago Peninsula, looking down the Otago Harbour, Dunedin

Morning on Tomahawk Beach, Otago Peninsula, Dunedin

The Dunedin Railway Station, built in 1906, and one of the
best-known historic buildings in the South Island

The Cadbury chocolate and confectionery factory, Dunedin

Autumn in the Wakatipu Basin, with The Remarkables behind, Queenstown

A view of Queenstown, with The Remarkables and Lake Wakatipu

The vintage steamship TSS *Earnslaw* arriving at Walter Peak Station,
from Queenstown, Lake Wakatipu

Sunset on Cecil Peak, Lake Wakatipu, Queenstown

The historic main street of Arrowtown, Central Otago

The restored bakehouse in the old goldmining settlement
of Macetown, Central Otago

The world famous Shotover Jet, operating on the Shotover River, Queenstown

Autumn on the shores of Lake Wanaka, Central Otago

Jet boat at Glenorchy, at the head of Lake Wakatipu, Otago

Swingbridge at the beginning of the Routeburn Track,
Mount Aspiring National Park

Remains of a goldminer's cottage in the historic reserve
at Bendigo, Central Otago

The man-made Blue Lake at St Bathans, Central Otago

An old schist farm building, Middlemarch, Central Otago

Autumn in the Ida Valley, Central Otago

Sea kayaks on Milford Sound, Fiordland National Park

Fishing boat tied up in Deepwater Basin, Milford Sound,
Fiordland National Park

Waterfalls near Homer Tunnel, Darren Mountains, Fiordland National Park

Cruising down Milford Sound, Fiordland National Park

Sunset, Milford Sound, Fiordland National Park

Last of the evening light, Milford Sound, Fiordland National Park

Nosing into the Stirling Falls, Milford Sound, Fiordland National Park

Stirling Falls, Milford Sound, Fiordland National Park

Sheepyards near Garston, Northern Southland

Paua shop, Riverton, Southland

The Gates of Haast, Haast Pass

Reeds and kahikatea forest, Lake Ianthe, Westland/Tai Poutini National Park

The western face of Mt Tasman, Westland/Tai Poutini National Park

Snowfall on the ranges near Haast, South Westland

Early morning on the track to Lake Matheson,
Westland/Tai Poutini National Park

Lake Matheson, Westland/Tai Poutini National Park

Terminal of the Franz Josef Glacier, Westland/Tai Poutini National Park

Peters Pool, a small kettle lake below the Franz Josef Glacier,
Westland/Tai Poutini National Park

Sea kayak on the shores of Okarito Lagoon, South Westland

Morning light on the Oparara River, near Karamea, Kahurangi National Park

Coastline near Tauranga Bay, Buller, West Coast

Kahikatea forest at Lake Brunner, Westland

Waves breaking at Dolomite Point, Punakaiki, Paparoa National Park

Pancake Rocks at Dolomite Point, Punakaiki, Paparoa National Park

Nikau palms above the Kohaihai River, southern end of the Heaphy Track, Kahurangi National Park

The Mirror Tarn, Oparara Basin, near Karamea, Kahurangi National Park